PIANO · VOCAL · GUITAR

100 Christmas Carols

ISBN 0-634-04756-6

HAL•LEONARD®
CORPORATION

7777 W. BLUEMOUND RD. P.O. BOX 13819 MILWAUKEE, WI 53213

In Australia Contact:
Hal Leonard Australia Pty. Ltd.
22 Taunton Drive P.O. Box 5130
Cheltenham East, 3192 Victoria, Australia
Email: ausadmin@halleonard.com

Visit Hal Leonard Online at
www.halleonard.com

contents

ANGELS FROM HEAVEN

Traditional Hungarian

AS EACH HAPPY CHRISTMAS

Traditional

ANGELS FROM
THE REALMS OF GLORY

Words by JAMES MONTGOMERY
Music by HENRY T. SMART

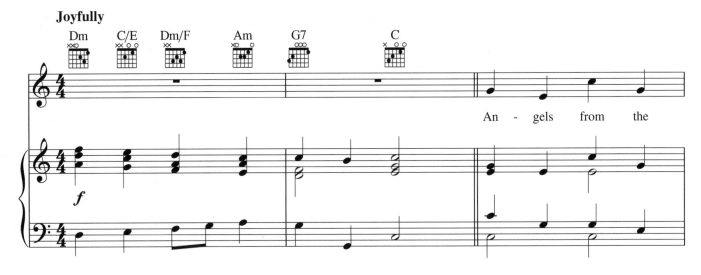

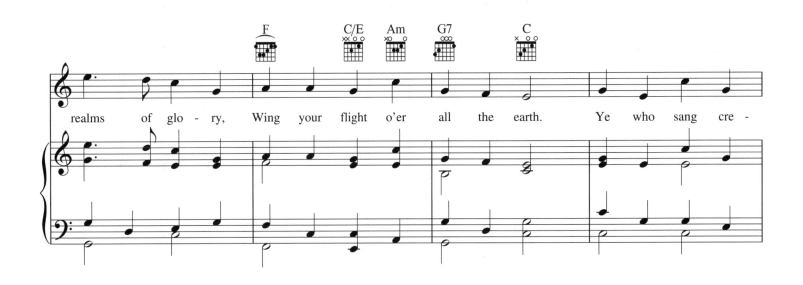

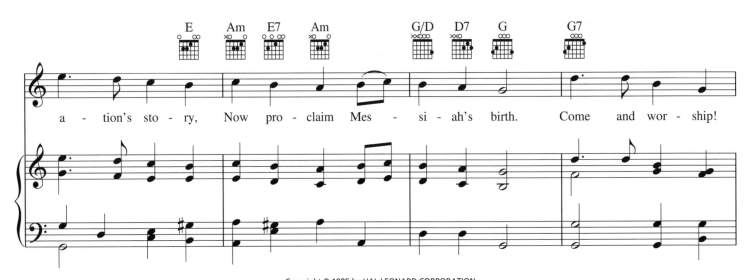

ANGELS WE HAVE HEARD ON HIGH

Traditional French Carol
Translated by JAMES CHADWICK

An - gels we have heard on high Sweet - ly sing - ing
Shep - herds, why this ju - bi - lee? Why your joy - ous

o'er the plains, And the moun - tains in re - ply
strains pro - long? What the glad - some tid - ings be

Ech - o - ing their joy - ous strains. } Glo -
Which in - spire your heav'n - ly song? }

AS LATELY WE WATCHED

19th Century Austrian Carol

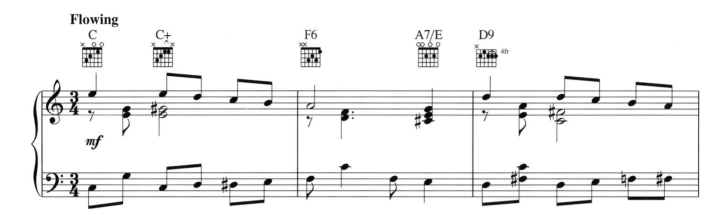

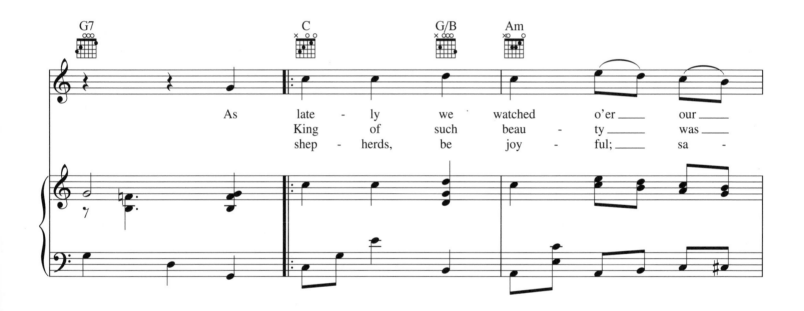

As late-ly we watched o'er our
King-ly of such beau-ty was
shep-herds, such be joy-ful; sa-

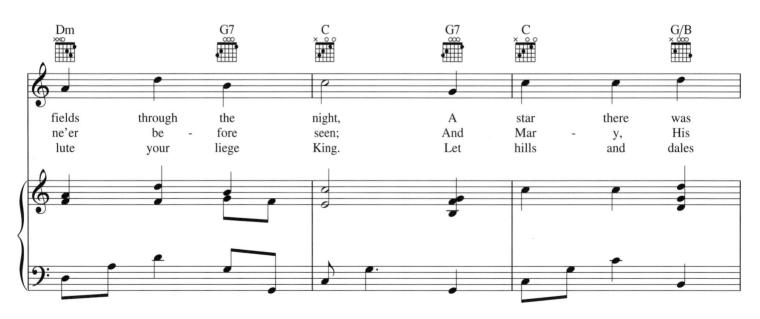

fields through the night, A star there was
ne'er be-fore seen; And Mar-y, His
lute be your liege King. Let hills and His dales

AS WITH GLADNESS MEN OF OLD

Words by WILLIAM CHATTERTON DIX
Music by CONRAD KOCHER

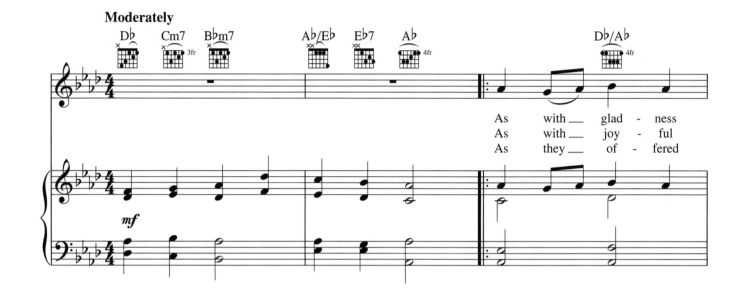

As with __ glad - ness
As with __ joy - ful
As they __ of - fered

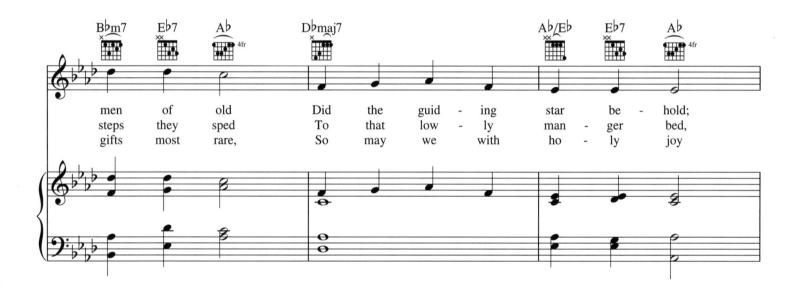

men of old, Did the guid - ing star be - hold;
steps they sped To that low - ly man - ger bed,
gifts most rare, So may we with ho - ly joy

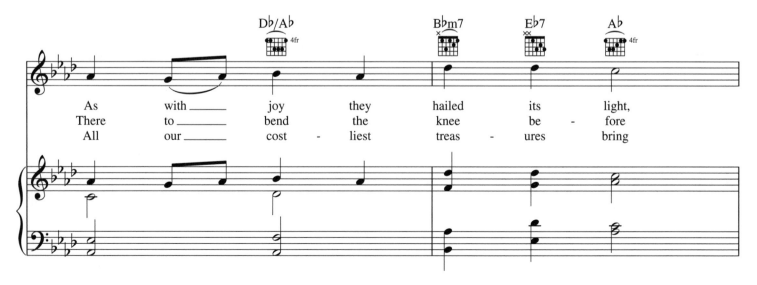

As with __ joy they hailed its light,
There to __ bend the knee be - fore
All our __ cost - liest treas - ures bring

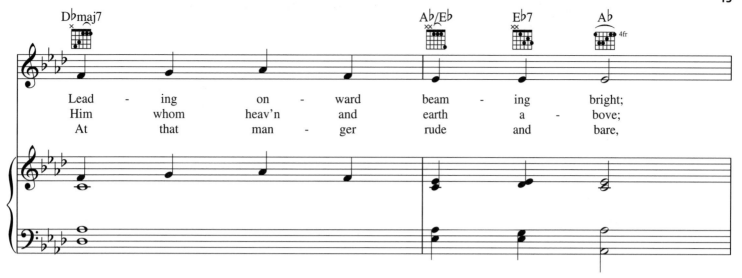

Lead - ing on - ward beam - ing bright;
Him whom on heav'n and earth a - bove;
At that man - ger rude and bare,

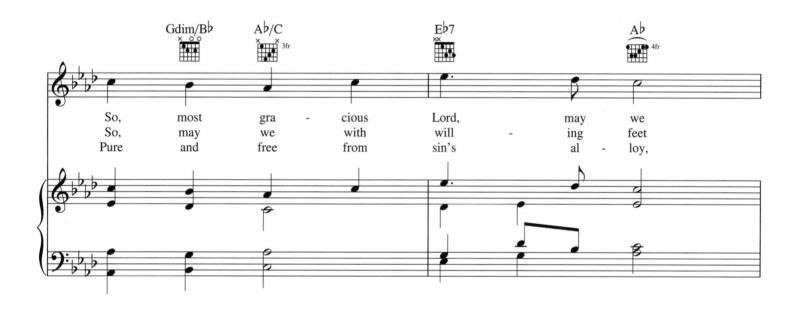

So, most gra - cious Lord, may we
So, may we with will - ing feet
Pure and free from sin's al - loy,

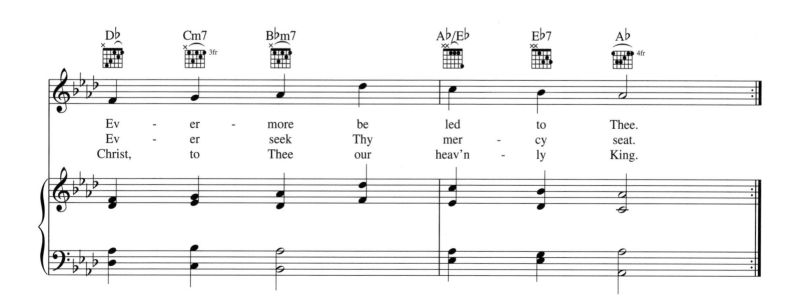

Ev - er - more be led to Thee.
Ev - er seek Thy mer - cy seat.
Christ, to Thee our heav'n - ly King.

AWAY IN A MANGER

Traditional Text
Words by JOHN T. McFARLAND (v.3)
Music by WILLIAM J. KIRKPATRICK

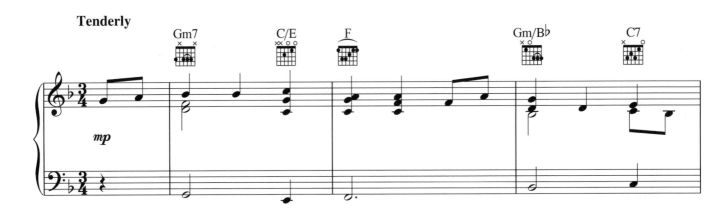

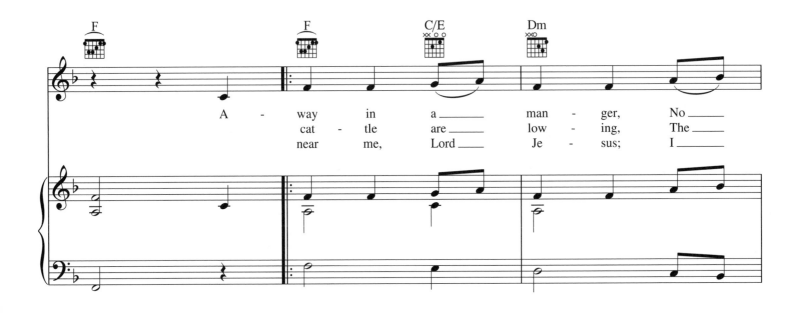

A - way in a _____ man - ger, No _____
cat - tle are _____ low - ing, The _____
near me, Lord _____ Je - sus; I _____

crib for a bed, The _____ lit - tle Lord
ba - by a - wakes, But _____ lit - tle Lord
ask Thee to stay Close _____ by me for -

AWAY IN A MANGER

Traditonal Text
Music by JAMES R. MURRAY

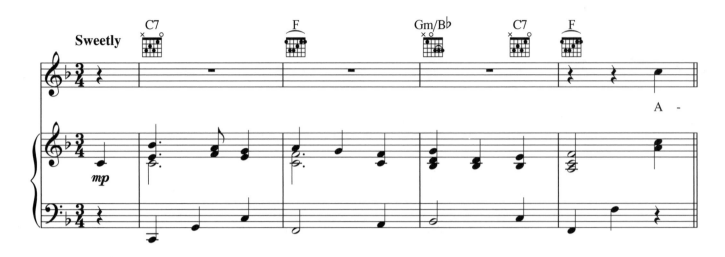

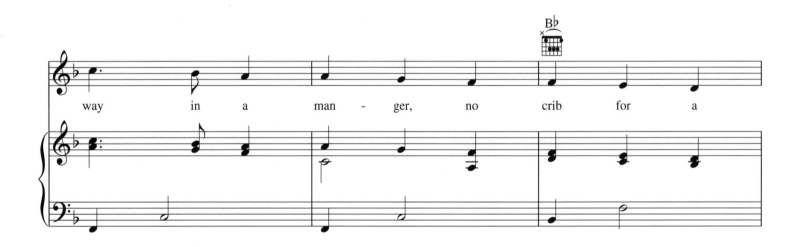

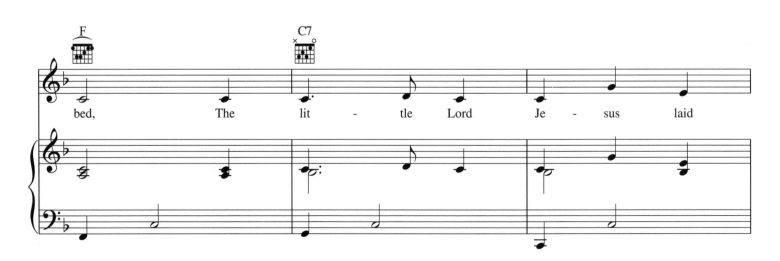

BELLS OVER BETHLEHEM

Traditional Andalucian Carol

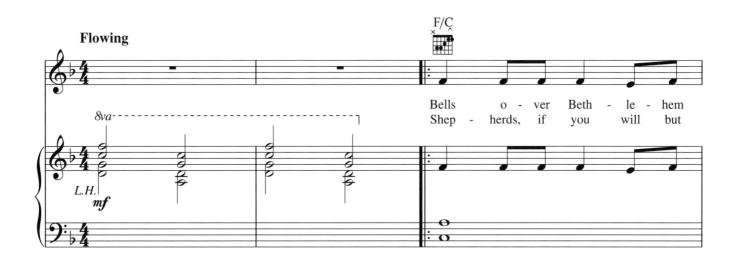

Bells o - ver Beth - le - hem
Shep - herds, if you will but

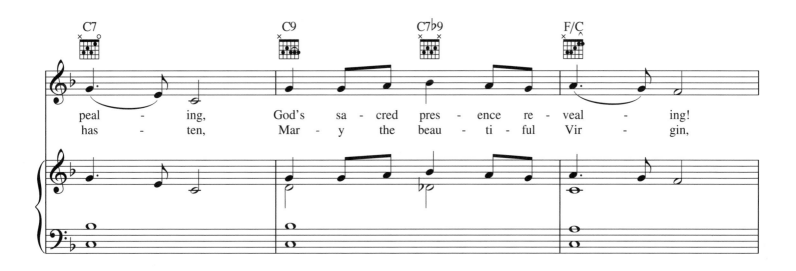

peal - ing, God's sa - cred pres - ence re - veal - ing!
has - ten, Mar - y the beau - ti - ful Vir - gin,

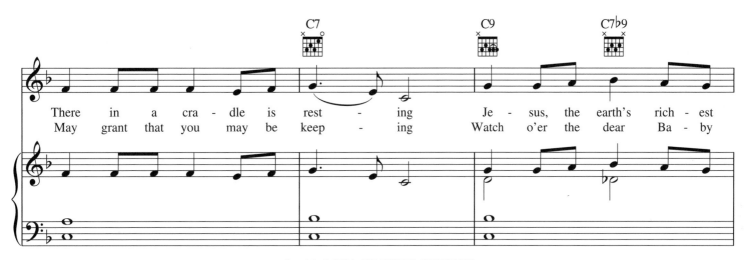

There in a cra - dle is rest - ing Je - sus, the earth's rich - est
May grant that you may be keep - ing Watch o'er the dear Ba - by

bless - ing!
sleep - ing.
The bells, the bells of Beth - le -

hem Are ring - ing out the tid - ings, "Good - will ___ to all

men!" Leave your sheep ___ and come, O shep - herds,

pres - ents bring the Babe so low - ly. ___

A BABY IN THE CRADLE

By D.G. CORNER

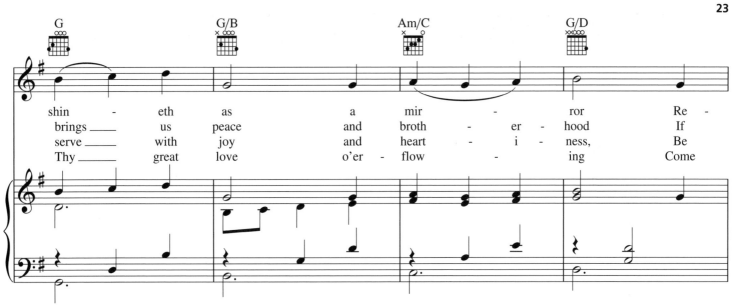

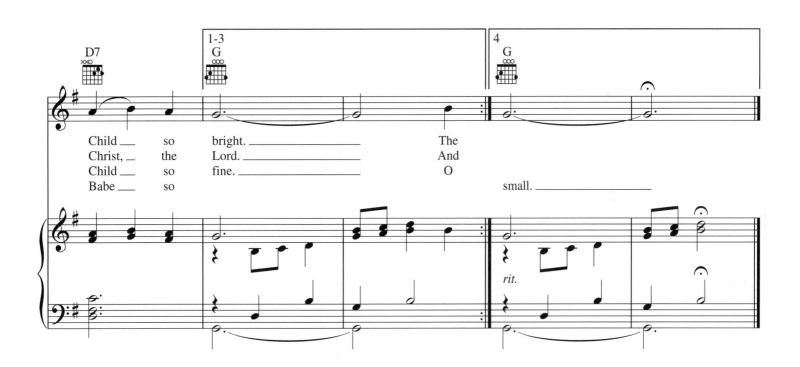

BESIDE THY CRADLE HERE I STAND

Words by PAUL GERHARDT
Translated by REV. J. TROUTBECK
Music from the *Geistliche Gesangbuch*

Slowly, with feeling

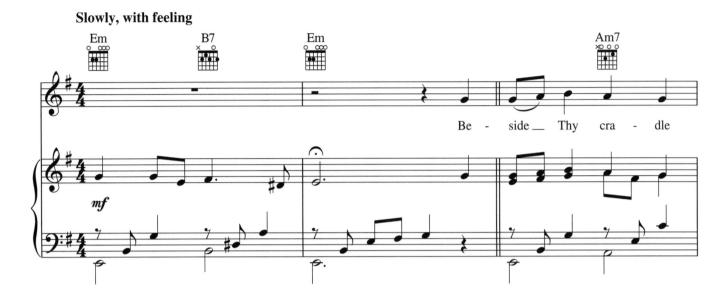

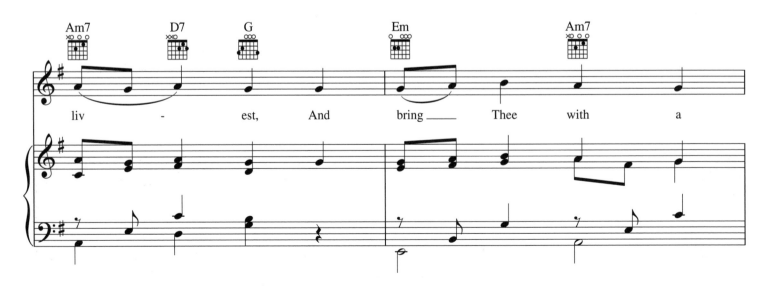

THE BOAR'S HEAD CAROL

Traditional English

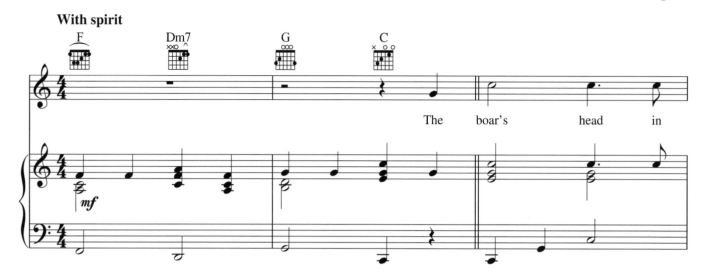

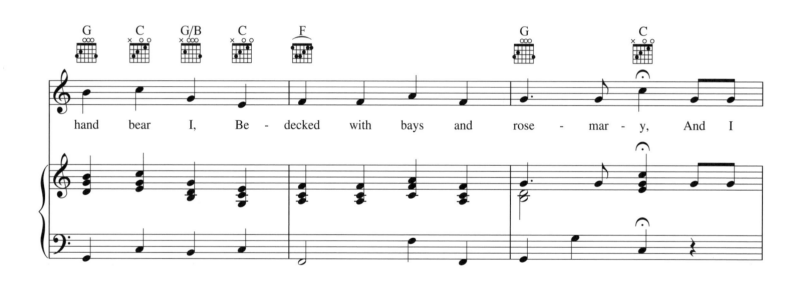

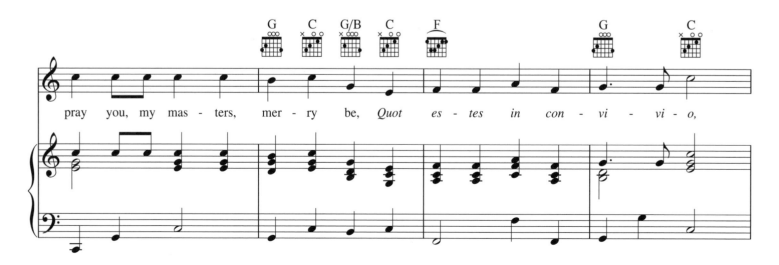

A BOY IS BORN IN BETHLEHEM

Traditional

BREAK FORTH, O BEAUTEOUS, HEAVENLY LIGHT

Words by JOHANN RIST
Translated by REV. J. TROUTBECK
Melody by JOHANN SCHOP

BRING A TORCH, JEANNETTE ISABELLA

17th Century French Provençal Carol

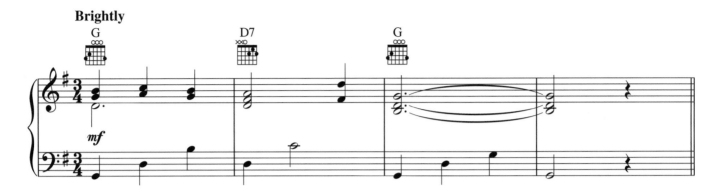

Bring a torch, ___ Jean-nette Is-a-bel-la,
Has-ten now, ___ good folk Is of the vil-lage,

Bring a torch, ___ come swift-ly and run.
Has-ten now, ___ come the Christ-ly Child to see.

33

CAROL OF THE BIRDS

Traditional Catalonian Carol

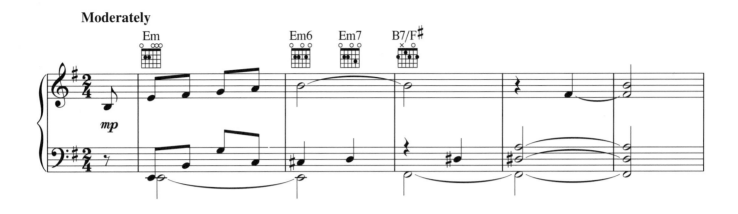

1. Up - on this ho - ly night, When God's great star ap - pears, And
2. night - in - gale is first To bring his song of cheer, And
3., 4. *(See additional verses)*

floods the earth with bright - ness Birds' voic - es rise in song, And
tell us of his glad - ness: Je - sus, our Lord, is born To

Additional Verses

3. The answ'ring Sparrow cries:
   "God comes to earth this day
   Amid the angels flying."
   Trilling in sweetest tones,
   The Finch his Lord now owns:
   "To Him be all thanksgiving."
   Trilling in sweetest tones,
   The Finch his Lord now owns:
   "To Him be all thanksgiving."

4. The Partridge adds his note:
   "To Bethlehem I'll fly,
   Where in the stall He's lying.
   There, near the manger blest,
   I'll build myself a nest,
   And sing my love undying.
   There, near the manger blest,
   I'll build myself a nest,
   And sing my love undying."

A CHILD IS BORN IN BETHLEHEM

14th-Century Latin Text adapted by
NICOLAI F.S. GRUNDTVIG
Traditional Danish Melody

THE CHRISTMAS TREE WITH ITS CANDLES GLEAMING

Traditional Czech Text
Traditional Bohemian-Czech Tune

CHILD JESUS CAME TO EARTH THIS DAY

Traditional Carol

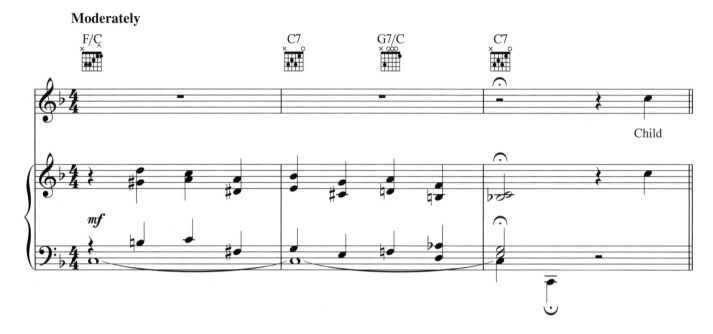

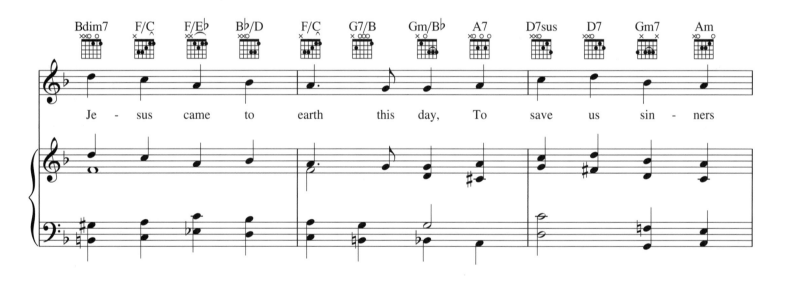

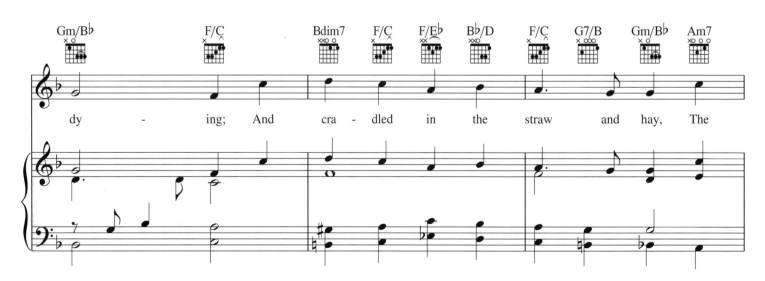

39

CHRIST IS BORN THIS EVENING

Traditional

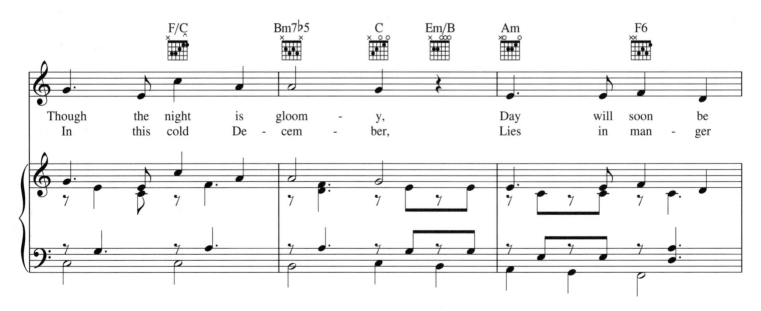

CHRIST WAS BORN
ON CHRISTMAS DAY

Traditional

Lilting

mf

Christ was born on Christ-mas day,

Wreath the hol-ly, twine the bay;

Christ - us na - tus ho - di - e; The Babe, the Son, the

CHRISTIANS, AWAKE! SALUTE THE HAPPY MORN

Traditional

COME, ALL YE SHEPHERDS

Traditional Czech Text
Traditional Moravian Melody

Lyrics:
Come, all ye shep-herds, such won-ders en-thrall. Come where the young Child is laid in a stall. This day to us a Sav-ior is giv-en, Whom God on high hath sent down from heav-en; Hal-le-lu-jah!

COME, THOU LONG-EXPECTED JESUS

Words by CHARLES WESLEY
Music by ROWLAND HUGH PRICHARD

48

COVENTRY CAROL

Words by ROBERT CROO
Traditional English Melody

Additional Verses

3. Herod the king,
   In his raging,
   Charged he hath this day.
   His men of might,
   In his own sight,
   All young children to slay.

4. That woe is me,
   Poor child for thee!
   And ever morn and day,
   For thy parting
   Neither say nor sing
   By by, lully lullay!

DANCE OF THE SUGAR PLUM FAIRY

from THE NUTCRACKER

By PYOTR IL'YICH TCHAIKOVSKY

A DAY, BRIGHT DAY OF GLORY

Traditional

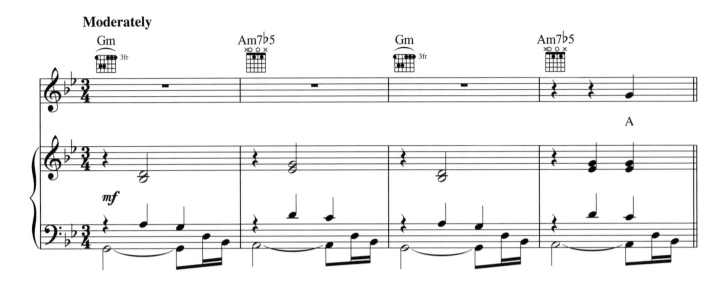

day, bright day of glo - ry! Glad day that ends our

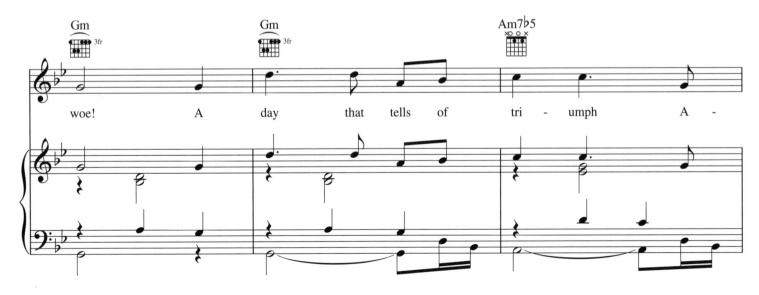

woe! A day that tells of tri - umph A -

DECK THE HALL

Traditional Welsh Carol

55

la la la. Don we now our gay ap - par - el,
la la la. Fol - low me in mer - ry meas - ure,
la la la. Sing we joy - ous all to - geth - er

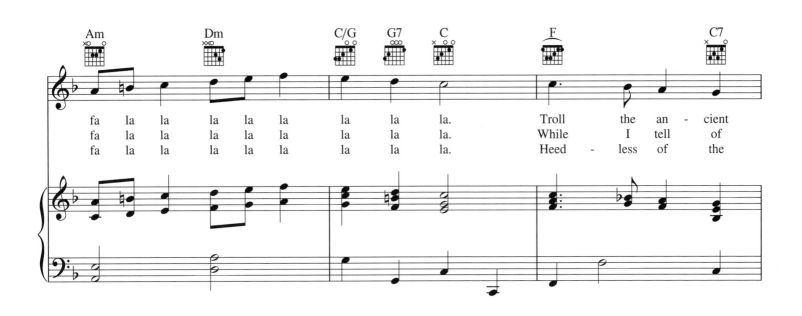

fa la la la la la la la la. Troll the an - cient
fa la la la la la la la la. While I tell of
fa la la la la la la la la. Heed - less of the

Yule - tide car - ol. Fa la la la la, la la la la
Yule - tide treas - ure. Fa la la la la, la la la la
wind and weath - er. Fa la la la la, la la la la

DING DONG! MERRILY ON HIGH!

French Carol

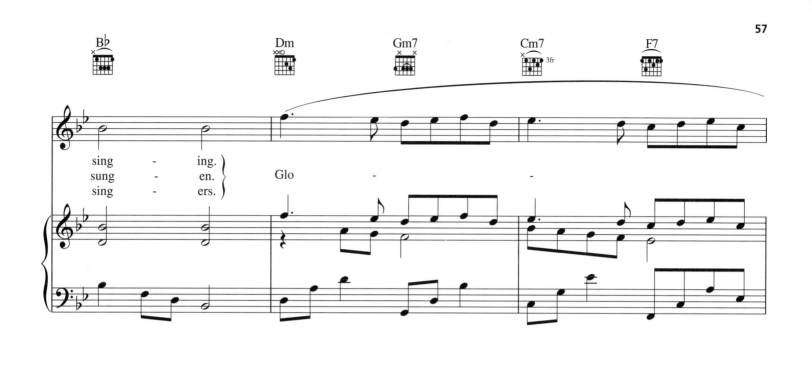

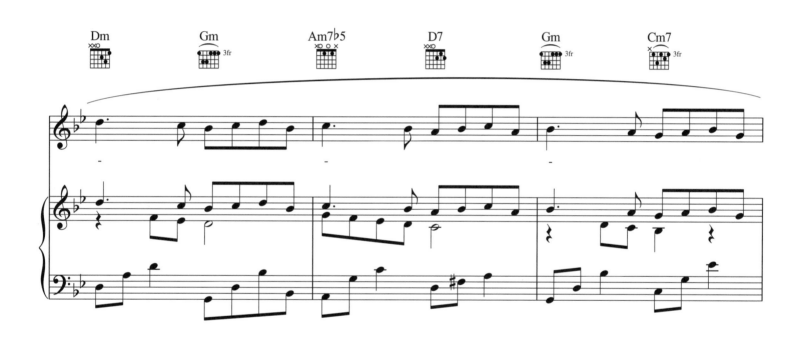

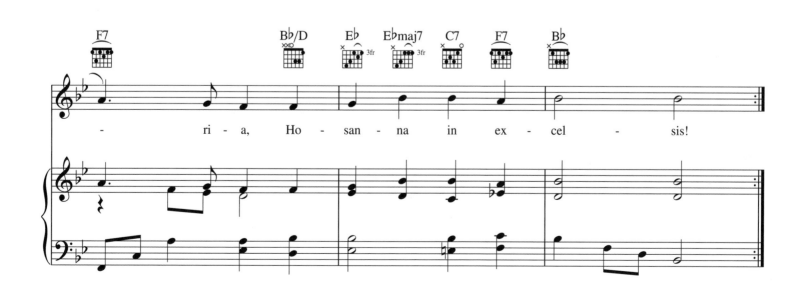

THE FIRST NOËL

17th Century English Carol
Music from W. Sandys' *Christmas Carols*

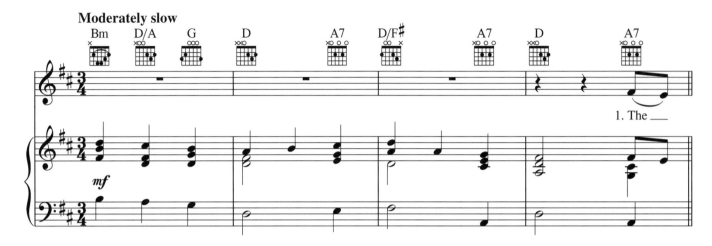

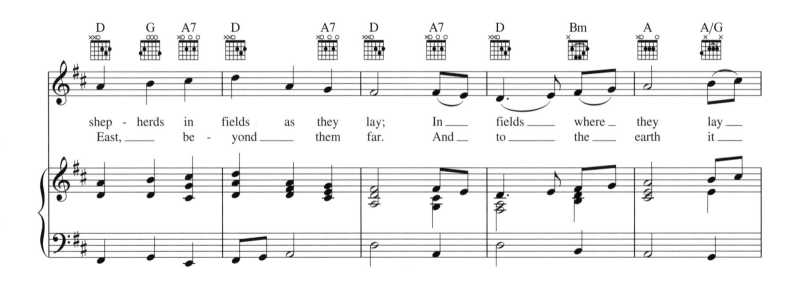

Additional Verses

3. And by the light of that same star,
   Three wise men came from country far.
   To seek for a King was their intent,
   And to follow the star wherever it went.
   Refrain

4. This star drew nigh to the northwest;
   O'er Bethlehem it took its rest.
   And there it did both stop and stay,
   Right over the place where Jesus lay.
   Refrain

5. Then entered in those wise men three,
   Full rev'rently upon their knee;
   And offered there in His presence,
   Their gold and myrrh and frankincense.
   Refrain

6. Then let us all with one accord
   Sing praises to our heav'nly Lord,
   That hath made heav'n and earth of naught,
   And with His blood mankind hath bought.
   Refrain

THE FRIENDLY BEASTS

Traditional English Carol

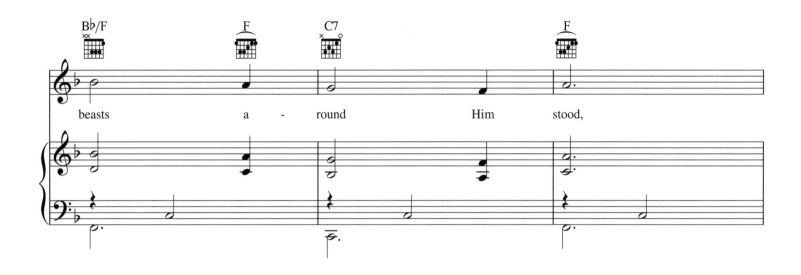

beasts a - round Him stood,

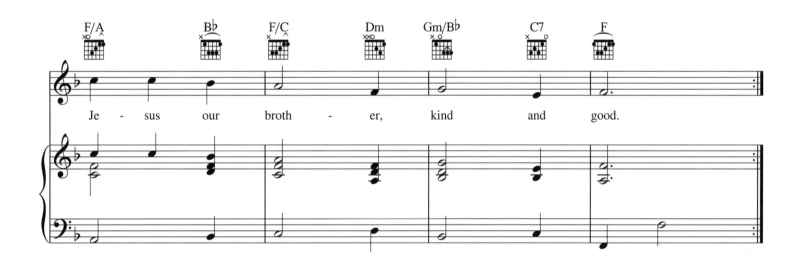

Je - sus our broth - er, kind and good.

Additional Verses

2. "I," said the donkey, shaggy and brown,
   "I carried His mother up hill and down;
   I carried her safely to Bethlehem town."
   "I," said the donkey, shaggy and brown.

3. "I," said the cow all white and red,
   "I gave Him my manger for His bed;
   I gave him my hay to pillow His head."
   "I," said the cow all white and red.

4. "I," said the sheep with curly horn,
   "I gave Him my wool for His blanket warm;
   He wore my coat on Christmas morn."
   "I," said the sheep with curly horn.

5. "I," said the dove from the rafters high,
   "I cooed Him to sleep so He would not cry;
   We cooed Him to sleep, my mate and I."
   "I," said the dove from the rafters high.

6. Thus every beast by some good spell,
   In the stable dark was glad to tell
   Of the gift he gave Emmanuel,
   The gift he gave Emmanuel.

FROM HEAVEN ABOVE TO EARTH I COME

Words and Music by
MARTIN LUTHER

FUM, FUM, FUM

Traditional Catalonian Carol

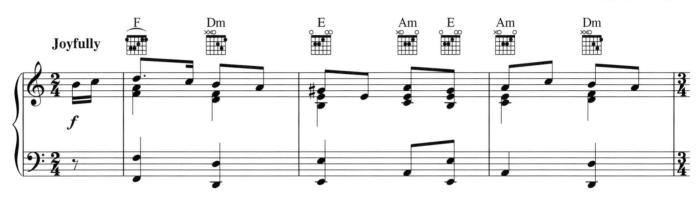

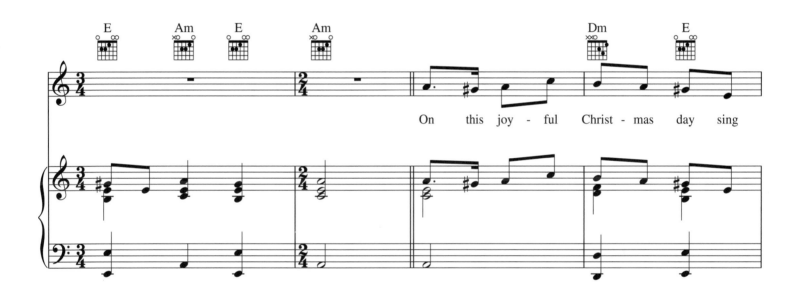

On this joy - ful Christ - mas day sing

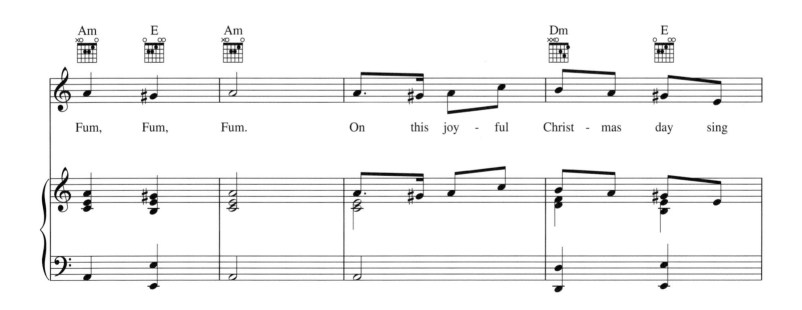

Fum, Fum, Fum. On this joy - ful Christ - mas day sing

GO, TELL IT ON THE MOUNTAIN

African-American Spiritual
Verses by JOHN W. WORK, JR.

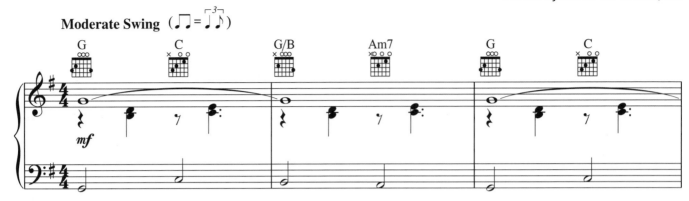

Moderate Swing

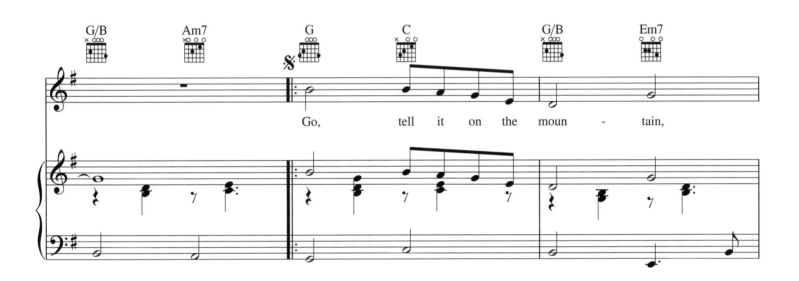

Go, tell it on the moun - tain,

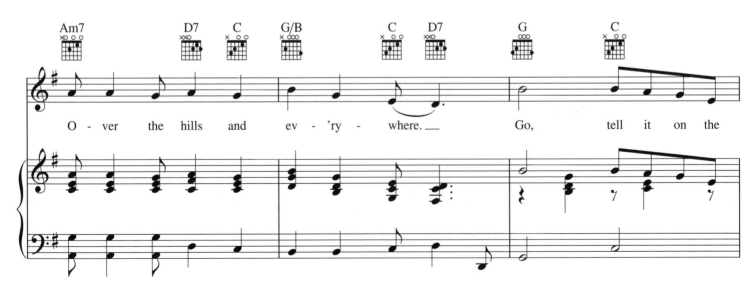

O - ver the hills and ev - 'ry - where. Go, tell it on the

GOD REST YE MERRY, GENTLEMEN

19th Century English Carol

God rest ye mer - ry, gen - tle - men, let
Beth - le - hem, in Jew - ry let this
God our Heav'n - ly Fa - ther A

noth - ing you dis - may, For Je - sus Christ our
bless - ed Babe was born, And laid with - in a
bless - ed an - gel came, And un - to cer - tain

Sav - ior was born up - on this day, To
man - ger, Up - on this bless - ed morn; To
shep - herds brought tid - ings of the same; How

GOOD CHRISTIAN MEN, REJOICE

14th Century Latin Text
Translated by JOHN MASON NEALE
14th Century German Melody

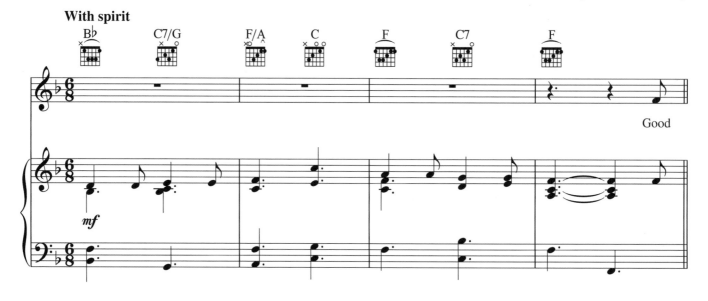

Chris - tian men, re - joice _____ with heart and soul and
Chris - tian men, re - joice _____ with heart and soul and

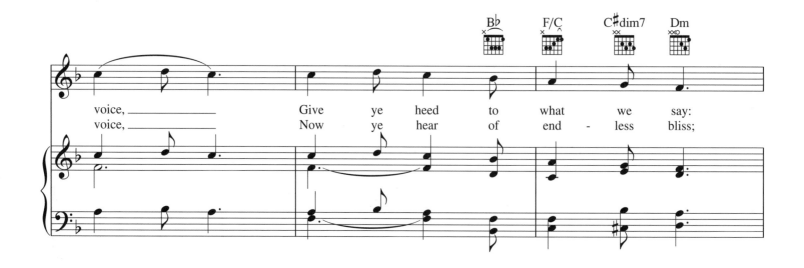

voice, _____ Give ye heed to what we say:
voice, _____ Now ye hear of end - less bliss;

GOOD KING WENCESLAS

Words by JOHN M. NEALE
Music from *Piae Cantiones*

With spirit

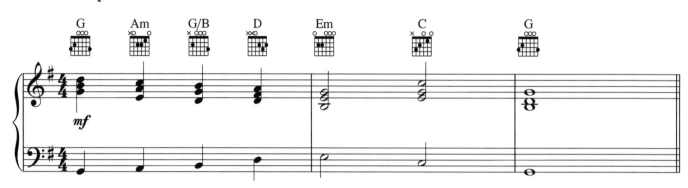

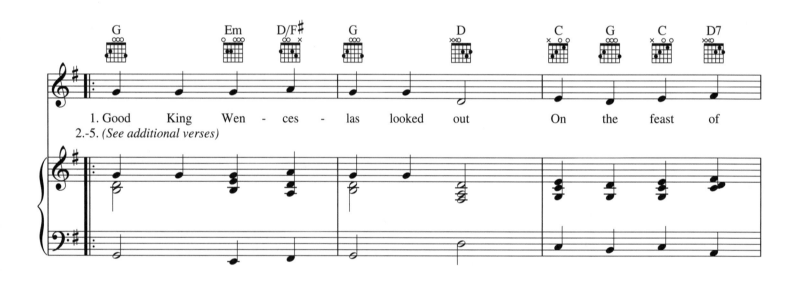

1. Good King Wen - ces - las looked out On the feast of
2.-5. *(See additional verses)*

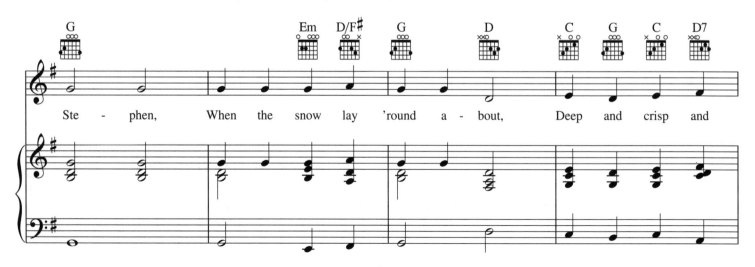

Ste - phen, When the snow lay 'round a - bout, Deep and crisp and

73

Additional Verses

2. "Hither page, and stand by me,
If thou know'st it, telling,
Yonder peasant, who is he?
Where and what his dwelling?"
"Sire, he lives a good league hence,
Underneath the mountain;
Right against the forest fence,
By Saint Agnes' fountain."

3. "Bring me flesh, and bring me wine,
Bring me pine-logs hither;
Thou and I will see him dine,
When we bear them thither."
Page and monarch forth they went,
Forth they went together;
Through the rude winds wild lament:
And the bitter weather.

4. "Sire, the night is darker now,
And the wind blows stronger;
Fails my heart, I know not how,
I can go no longer."
"Mark my footsteps, my good page,
Tred thou in them boldly:
Thou shalt find the winter's rage
Freeze thy blood less coldly."

5. In his master's steps he trod,
Where the snow lay dinted;
Heat was in the very sod
Which the saint had printed.
Therefore, Christian men, be sure,
Wealth or rank possessing,
Ye who now will bless the poor,
Shall yourselves find blessing.

THE HAPPY CHRISTMAS COMES ONCE MORE

Words by NICOLAI F.S. GRUNDTVIG
Music by C. BALLE

Flowing Waltz (not too fast)

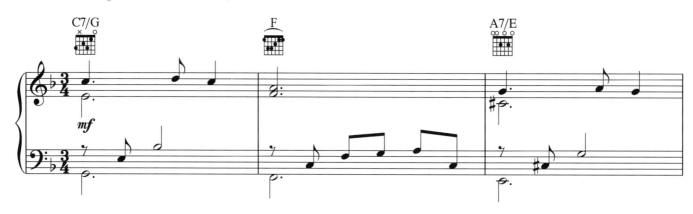

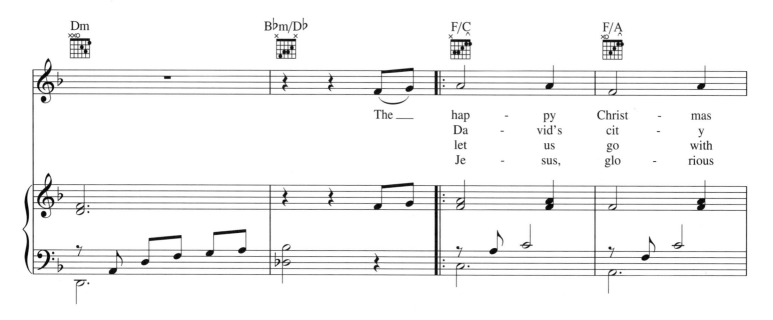

The hap - py Christ - mas
Da - vid's cit - y
Je - sus, glo - rious

comes once more, The heav'n - ly Guest is
let us fly, Where an - gels sing be -
qui - et mind, The gen - tle Babe with
heav'n - ly Guest, Keep Thine own Christ - mas

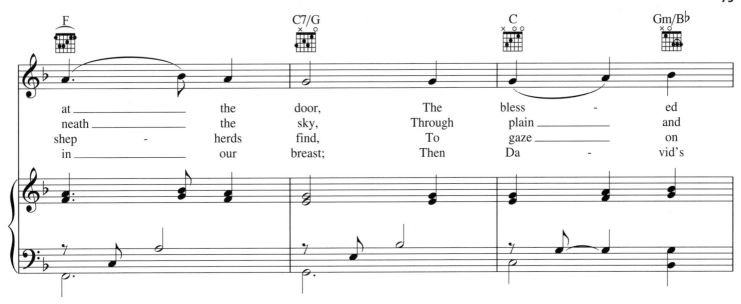

at _____ the door, The bless - ed
neath _____ the sky, Through plain _____ and
shep - herds find, To gaze _____ on
in _____ our breast; Then Da - vid's

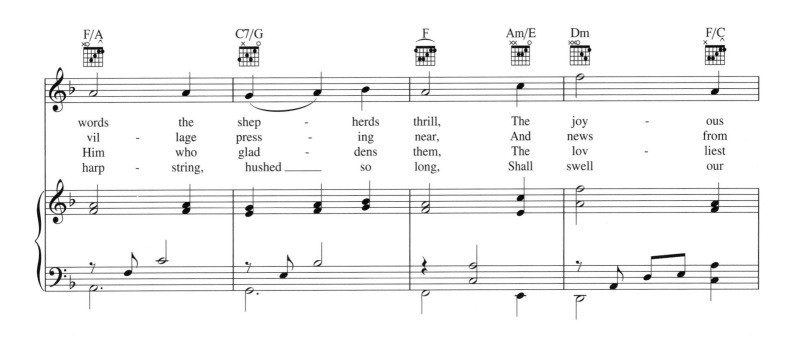

words the shep - herds thrill, The joy - ous
vil - lage press - ing near, And news from
Him who glad - dens them, The lov - liest
harp - string, hushed _____ so long, Shall swell our

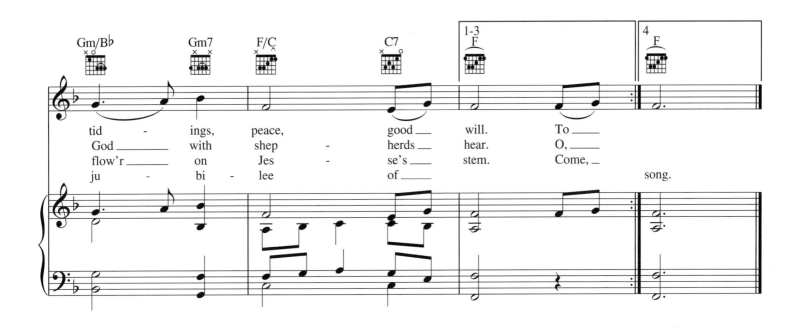

tid - ings, peace, good ___ will. To ___
God _____ with shep - herds ___ hear. O, ___
flow'r _____ on Jes - se's ___ stem. Come, ___
ju - bi - lee of ___ song.

HARK! THE HERALD ANGELS SING

Words by CHARLES WESLEY
Altered by GEORGE WHITEFIELD
Music by FELIX MENDELSSOHN-BARTHOLDY

Hark! The her - ald an - gels sing,____
Christ, by high - est heav'n a - dored,____
Hail, the heav'n - born Prince of Peace!____

"Glo - ry to the new - born King!
Christ, the ev - er - last - ing Lord;
Hail, the Sun of Right - eous - ness!

Peace on earth, and
Late in time be -
Light and life to

mer - cy mild,____ God and sin - ners rec - on - ciled."
hold Him come,____ Off - spring of the vir - gin's womb.
all He brings,____ Ris'n with heal - ing in His wings.

HE IS BORN, THE HOLY CHILD

Traditional French Carol

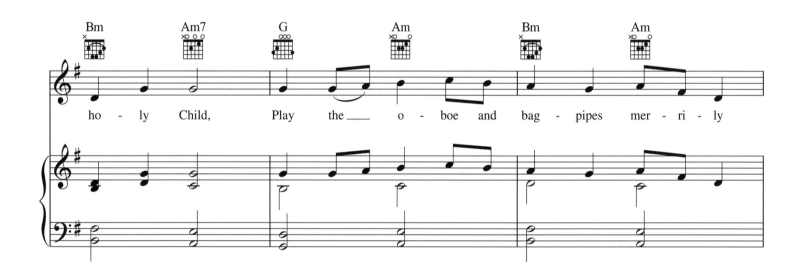

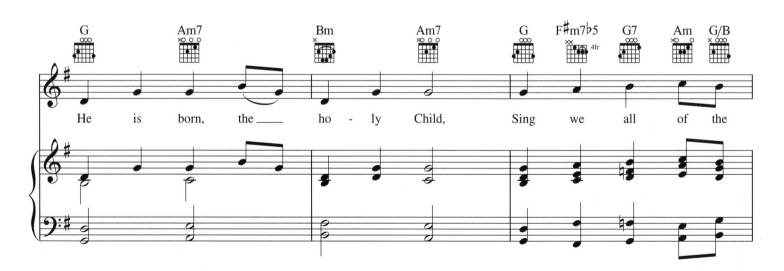

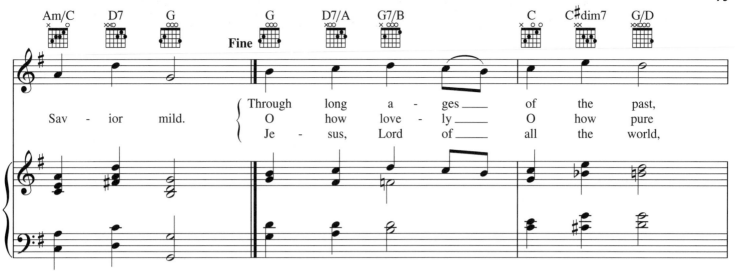

Sav - ior mild.

{ Through long a - ges ___ of the past,
O how love - ly ___ O how pure
Je - sus, Lord of ___ all the world,

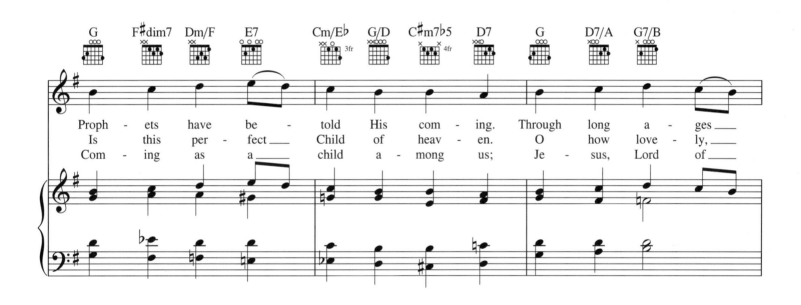

Proph - ets have be - told His com - ing. Through long a - ges ___
Is this per - fect ___ Child of heav - en. O how love - ly, ___
Com - ing as a ___ child a - mong us; Je - sus, Lord of ___

of the past; Now the time has ___ come at last!
O how pure, Gra - cious gift of ___ God to man!
all the world, Grant to us Thy ___ heav'n - ly peace.

HERE WE COME A-WASSAILING

Traditional

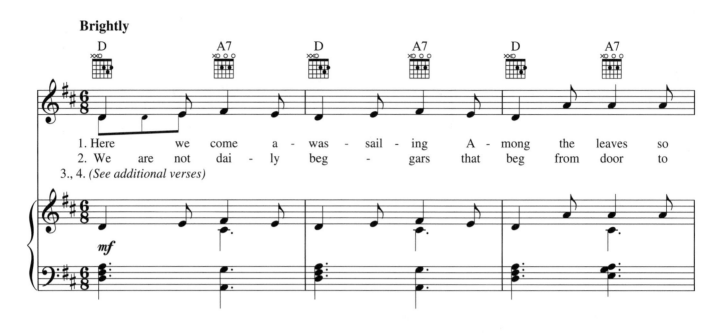

1. Here we come a-was-sail-ing A-mong the leaves so
2. We are not dai-ly beg-gars that beg from door to
3., 4. *(See additional verses)*

green; Here we come a-wan-d'ring, So fair _____ to be
door, But we are neigh-bor chil-dren whom you have seen be-

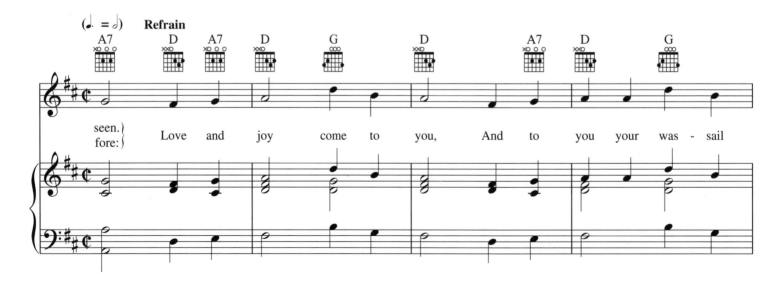

seen.}
fore:} Love and joy come to you, And to you your was-sail

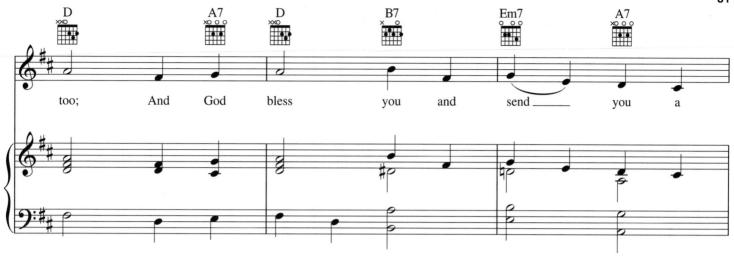

too; And God bless you and send _____ you a

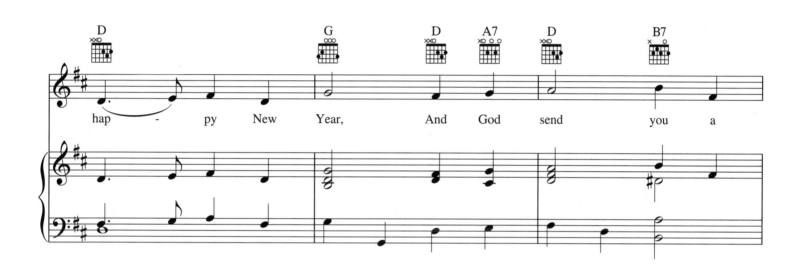

hap - py New Year, And God send you a

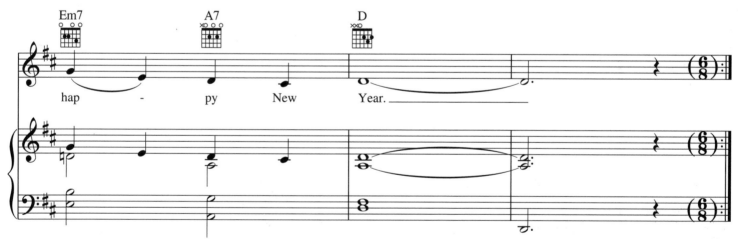

hap - py New Year. _____

Additional Verses

3. We have got a little purse
   Of stretching leather skin;
   We want a little money
   To line it well within:
   Refrain

4. God bless the master of this house,
   Likewise the mistress too;
   And all the little children
   That round the table go:
   Refrain

THE HOLLY AND THE IVY

18th Century English Carol

I AM SO GLAD ON CHRISTMAS EVE

Words by MARIE WEXELSEN
Music by PEDER KNUDSEN

I HEARD THE BELLS ON CHRISTMAS DAY

Words by HENRY WADSWORTH LONGFELLOW
Music by JOHN BAPTISTE CALKIN

Additional Verses

3. And in despair I bowed my head:
   "There is no peace on earth," I said,
   "For hate is strong, and mocks the song
   Of peace on earth, good will to men."

4. Then pealed the bells more loud and deep:
   "God is not dead, nor doth He sleep;
   The wrong shall fail, the right prevail,
   With peace on earth, good will to men."

5. Till, ringing, singing on its way,
   The world revolved from night to day,
   A voice, a chime, a chant sublime,
   Of peace on earth, good will to men!

I SAW THREE SHIPS

Traditional English Carol

IN THE FIELD WITH THEIR FLOCKS ABIDING

Traditional

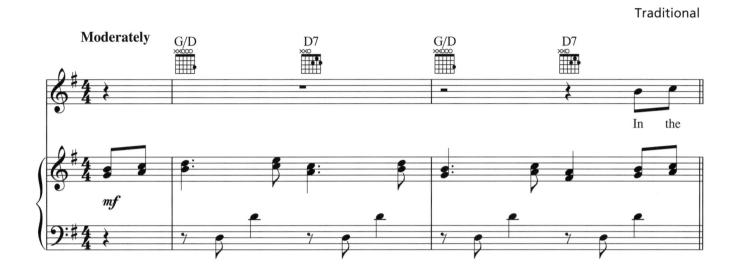

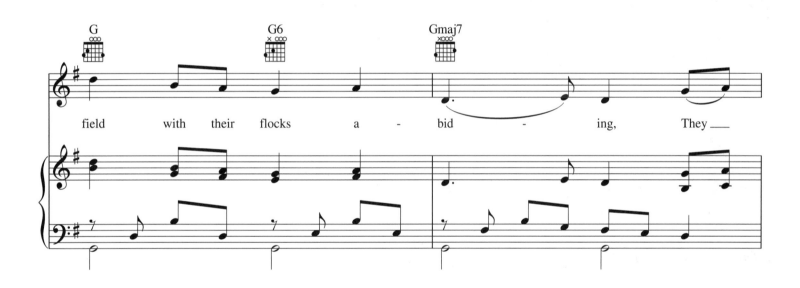

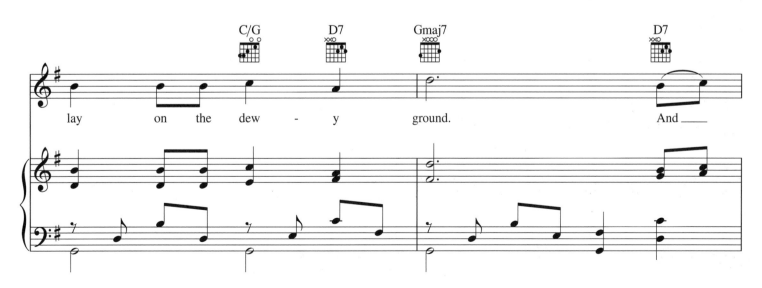

88

IN THE SILENCE OF THE NIGHT

Traditional Carol

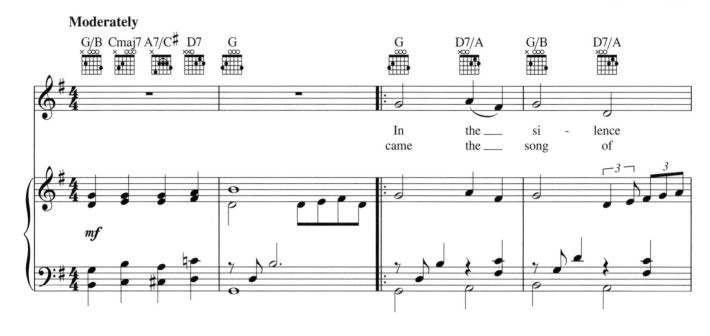

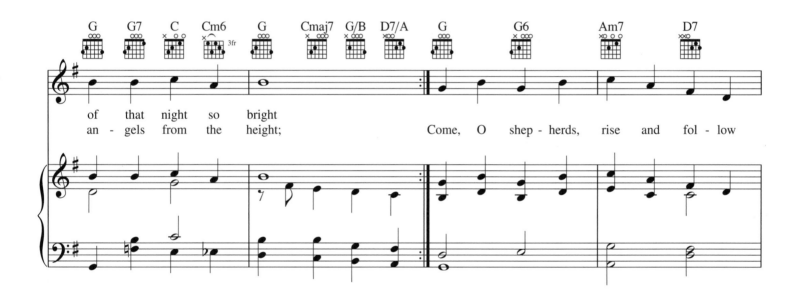

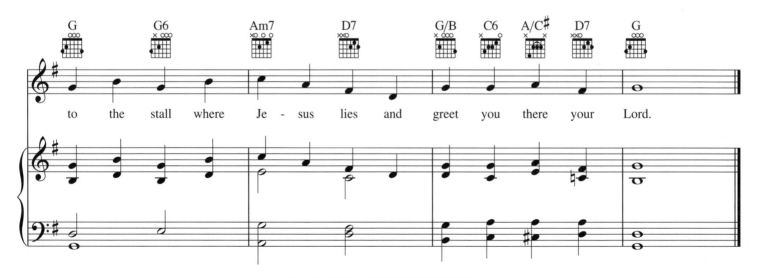

IT CAME UPON THE MIDNIGHT CLEAR

Words by EDMUND HAMILTON SEARS
Music by RICHARD STORRS WILLIS

92

JESU, JOY OF MAN'S DESIRING

By JOHANN SEBASTIAN BACH

MASTERS IN THIS HALL

Traditional English

Mas- ters in this hall, _____

Hear ye news to- day, _____ Brought from o- ver

sea, And ev- er I you pray.

JESUS HOLY, BORN SO LOWLY

Traditional Polish

JOY TO THE WORLD

Words by ISAAC WATTS
Music by GEORGE FRIDERIC HANDEL
Arranged by LOWELL MASON

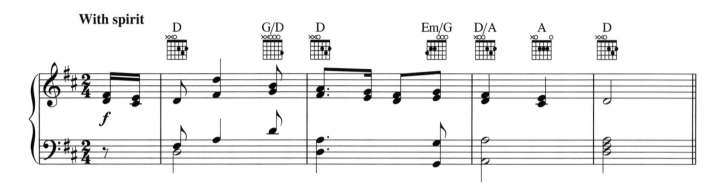

Joy to the world! The Lord is come; Let
Joy to the world! The earth! The Sav - ior reigns; Let
He rules the world with truth and grace, And

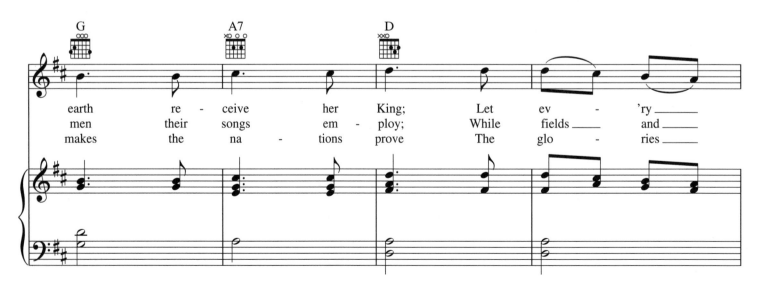

earth re - ceive her King; Let ev - 'ry
men their songs em - ploy; While fields and
makes the na - tions prove The glo - ries

heart _____ pre - pare ___ Him ___ room, _____ and heav'n and na - ture ___
floods, _____ rocks, hills and ___ plains _____ Re - peat the sound - ing ___
of _____ His right - eous - ness _____ And won - ders of His ___

A

sing, ___ And ___ heav'n and na - ture ___ sing, ___ And ___
joy, ___ Re - peat the sound - ing ___ joy, ___ Re -
love, ___ And ___ won - ders of His ___ love, ___ And ___

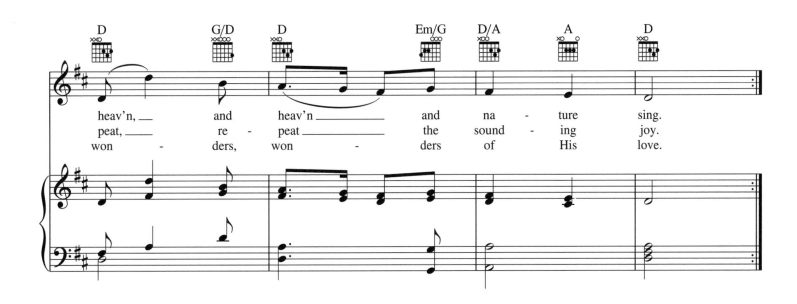

D   G/D   D   Em/G   D/A   A   D

heav'n, ___ and heav'n _____ and na - ture sing.
peat, ___ re - peat _____ the sound - ing joy.
won - ders, won - ders of His ___ love.

LO, HOW A ROSE E'ER BLOOMING

15th Century German Carol
Translated by THEODORE BAKER
Music from *Alte Catholische Geistliche Kirchengesäng*

NEIGHBOR, WHAT HAS YOU SO EXCITED?

Traditional French

NOËL! NOËL!

French-English Carol

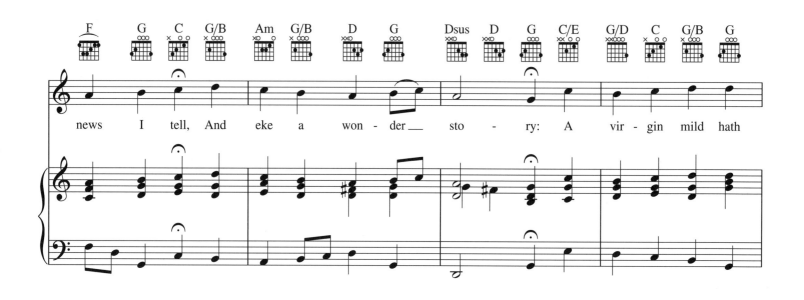

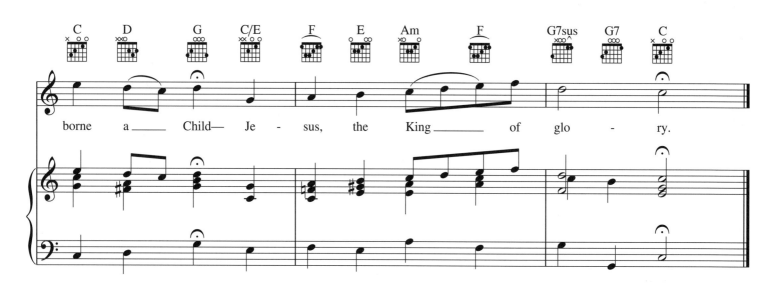

O COME, O COME, IMMANUEL

Plainsong, 13th Century
Words translated by JOHN M. NEALE
and HENRY S. COFFIN

Moderately slow, in 2

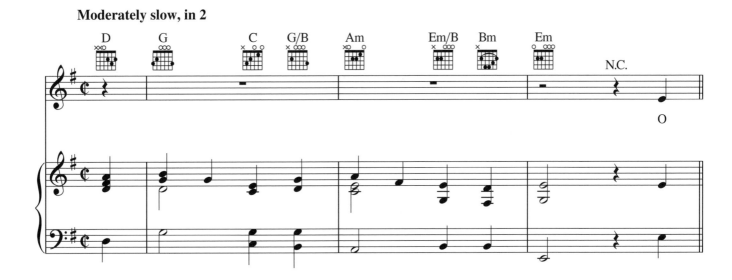

O

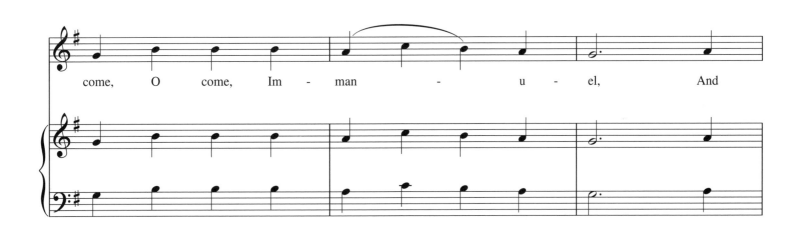

come, O come, Im - man - u - el, And

ran - som cap - tive Is - ra - el, That mourns in lone - ly

112

O BETHLEHEM

Traditional Spanish

O CHRISTMAS TREE

Traditional German Carol

O Christ - mas tree! O Christ - mas tree, you
Christ - mas tree! O Christ - mas tree, much
Christ - mas tree! O Christ - mas tree, thy

stand in ver - dant beau - ty! O Christ - mas tree, O
pleas - ure doth thou bring me! O Christ - mas tree, O
can - dles shine out bright - ly! O Christ - mas tree, O

Christ - mas tree, you stand in ver - dant beau - ty! Your
Christ - mas tree, much pleas - ure doth thou bring me! For
Christ - mas tree, thy can - dles shine out bright - ly! Each

O COME, ALL YE FAITHFUL

Words and Music by JOHN FRANCIS WADE
Latin Words translated by FREDERICK OAKELEY

119

O COME AWAY, YE SHEPHERDS

18th Century French Text
Tune from Air, "Nanon Dormait"

O COME, LITTLE CHILDREN

Words by C. VON SCHMIDT
Music by J.P.A. SCHULZ

O COME REJOICING

Traditional Polish Carol

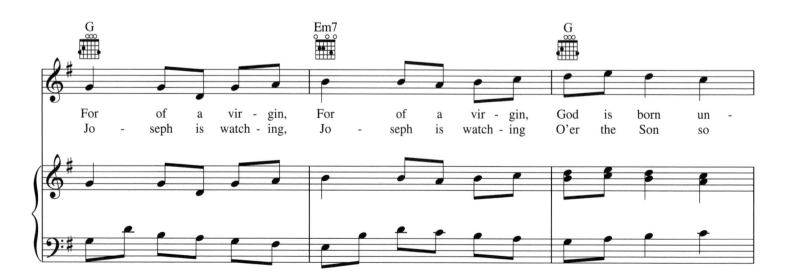

O HOLY NIGHT

French Words by PLACIDE CAPPEAU
English Words by JOHN S. DWIGHT
Music by ADOLPHE ADAM

O LET US ALL BE GLAD TODAY

Words and Music by
MARTIN LUTHER

Additional Verses

3. Twice welcome, O Thou heavenly guest,
   To save a world with sin distressed;
   Com'st Thou in lowly guise for me?
   What homage shall I give to Thee?

4. Ah! Lord eternal, heavenly King,
   Hast Thou become so mean a thing?
   And hast Thou left Thy blissful seat,
   To rest where colts and oxen eat?

5. Jesus, my Savior, come to me,
   Make here a little crib for Thee;
   A bed make in this heart of mine,
   That I may ay remember Thine.

6. Then from my soul glad songs shall ring;
   Of Thee each day I'll gladly sing;
   Then glad hosannas will I raise,
   From heart that loves to sing Thy praise.

RISE UP, SHEPHERD, AND FOLLOW

African-American Spiritual

O LITTLE TOWN OF BETHLEHEM

Words by PHILLIPS BROOKS
Music by LEWIS H. REDNER

O SANCTISSIMA

Sicilian Carol

Day of ho - li - ness, _____ peace and hap - pi - ness, _____

OF THE FATHER'S LOVE BEGOTTEN

Words by AURELIUS C. PRUDENTIUS
Translated by JOHN M. NEALE and HENRY W. BAKER
13th Century Plainsong

1. Of the Fa-ther's love be-
2. O that birth for-ev-er
3.-5. *(See additional verses)*

got- ten, Ere the worlds be-gan ___ to be,
bless -ed, When the vir-gin, full ___ of grace,

He is Al-pha and O-me-ga, He the Source, the End-ing
By the Ho-ly Ghost con-ceiv-ing, Bore the Sav-ior of our

Additional Verses

3. This is He whom seers in old time
   Chanted of with one accord,
   Whom the voices of the prophets
   Promised in their faithful word.
   Now He shines, the long-expected;
   Let creation praise its Lord
   Evermore and evermore!

4. Let the heights of heav'n adore Him;
   Angel hosts, His praises sing.
   Pow'rs, dominions, bow before Him
   And extol our God and King.
   Let no tongue on earth be silent;
   Ev'ry voice in concert ring
   Evermore and evermore!

5. Christ, to Thee, with God the Father,
   And, O Holy Ghost, to Thee,
   Hymn and chant and high thanksgiving
   And unwearied praises be:
   Honor, glory and dominion
   And eternal victory
   Evermore and evermore!

ON CHRISTMAS NIGHT

Sussex Carol

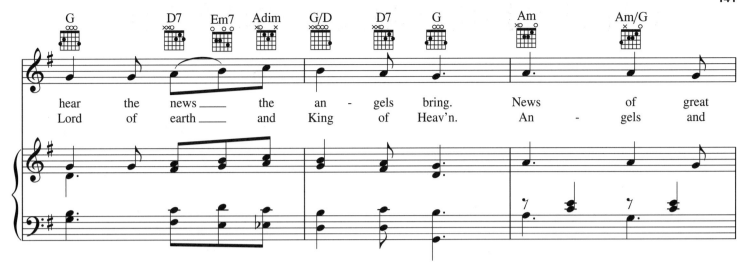

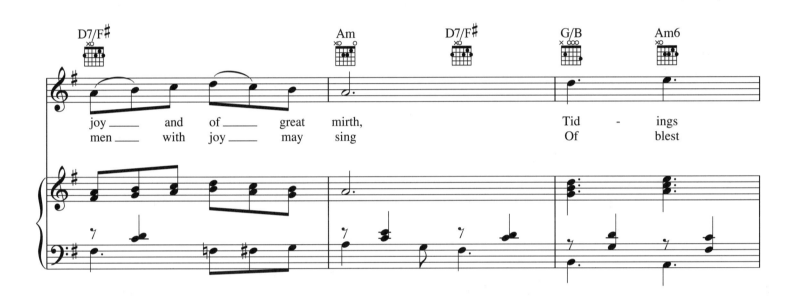

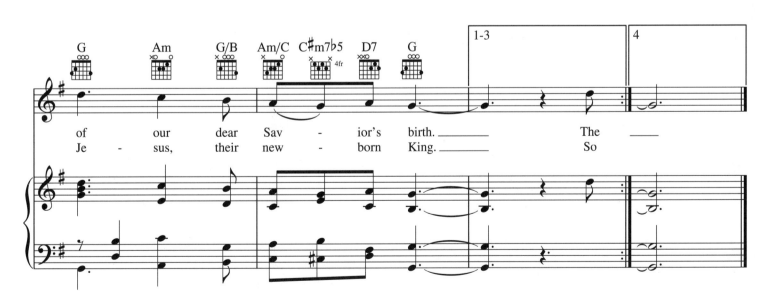

Additional Verses

3. So how on earth can men be sad,
   When Jesus comes to make us glad?
   So how on earth can men be sad,
   When Jesus comes to make us glad?
   From all our sins to set us free,
   Buying for us our liberty.

4. From out the darkness have we light,
   Which makes the angels sing this night.
   From out the darkness have we light,
   Which makes the angels sing this night:
   "Glory to God, His peace to men,
   And good will, evermore! Amen."

ONCE IN ROYAL DAVID'S CITY

Words by CECIL F. ALEXANDER
Music by HENRY J. GAUNTLETT

143

PAT-A-PAN
(Willie, Take Your Little Drum)

Words and Music by
BERNARD de la MONNOYE

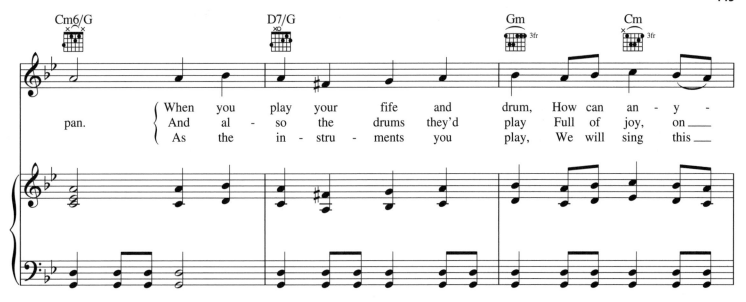

When you play your fife and drum, How can an - y -
And al - so the drums they'd play Full of joy, on ___
As the in - stru - ments you play, We will sing this ___

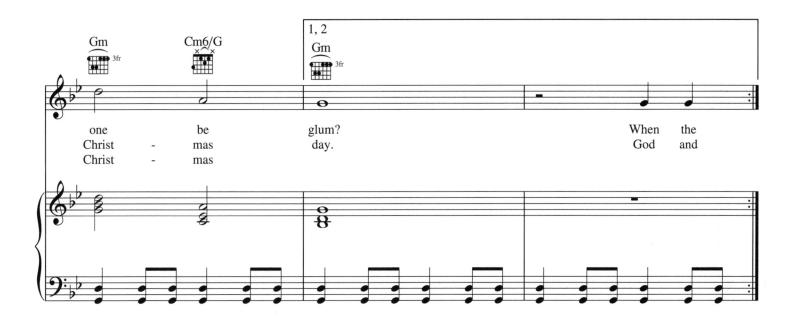

one be glum? When the
Christ - mas day. God and
Christ - mas

day.

REJOICE AND BE MERRY

Gallery Carol

Additional Verses

3. Likewise a bright star in the sky did appear,
   Which led the wise men from the east to draw near.
   They found the Messiah, sweet Jesus our King,
   Who brought us salvation; His praises we'll sing!

4. And when they were come, they their treasures unfold,
   And unto Him offered myrrh, incense, and gold.
   So blessed forever be Jesus our King,
   Who brought us salvation; His praises we'll sing!

RING OUT, YE WILD AND MERRY BELLS

Words and Music by
C. MAITLAND

Brightly

out, ye wild and mer-ry bells, Ring out __ the old __ old sto- __ ry That
out, ye sil - v'ry bells, ring out, Ring out __ your ex - ul - ta - tion That

first was told by an - gel tongues From out the realms of Glo- ry.
God with man is re - con - ciled. Go tell it to the na- tions.

SHEPHERD! SHAKE OFF YOUR DROWSY SLEEP

Traditional French Carol

Shep - herd! shake off your drows - y sleep; Rise and
flow'rs all burst a - new, Think - ing
up and quick a - way! Seek the

leave your sil - ly sheep. An - gels from
snow is sum - mer dew. See how from the
Babe ere break of day. He is the

SHEPHERD'S CRADLE SONG

Words and Music by
C.D. SCHUBERT

153

SING WE NOW OF CHRISTMAS

Traditional

SHOUT THE GLAD TIDINGS

Traditional

SILENT NIGHT

Words by JOSEPH MOHR
Translated by JOHN F. YOUNG
Music by FRANZ X. GRUBER

THE SIMPLE BIRTH

Traditional Flemish Carol

Additional Verses

3. His eyes of blackest jet were sparkling with light, *(Repeat)*
   Rosy cheeks bloomed on His face fair and bright. *(Repeat)*

4. And from His lovely mouth, the laughter did swell, *(Repeat)*
   When He saw Mary, whom He loved so well. *(Repeat)*

5. He came to weary earth, so dark and so drear, *(Repeat)*
   To wish mankind a blessed New Year. *(Repeat)*

SING, O SING, THIS BLESSED MORN

Words by CHRISTOPHER WORDSWORTH
Traditional German Tune

1. Sing, O sing, this bless-ed morn.
2. God with us, Im-man-u-el,
3., 4. (See additional verses)

Un-to us a Child is born, Un-to us a
Reigns for-e-ver now to dwell, And on A-dam's

165

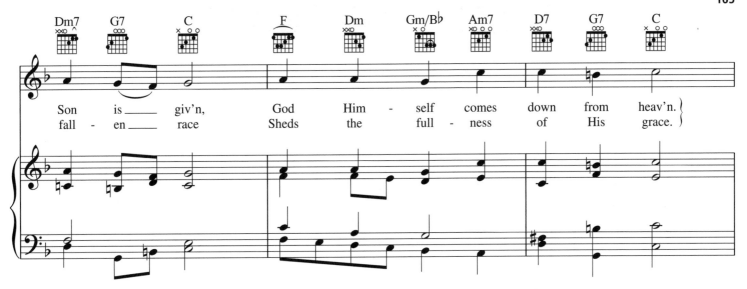

Son is __ giv'n, God Him - self comes down from heav'n.
fall - en __ race Sheds the full - ness of His grace.

Refrain

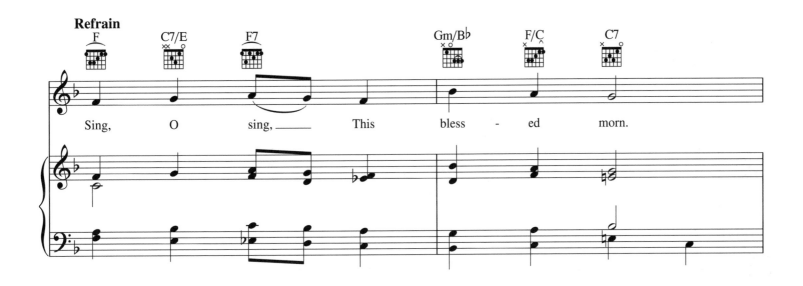

Sing, O sing, ____ This bless - ed morn.

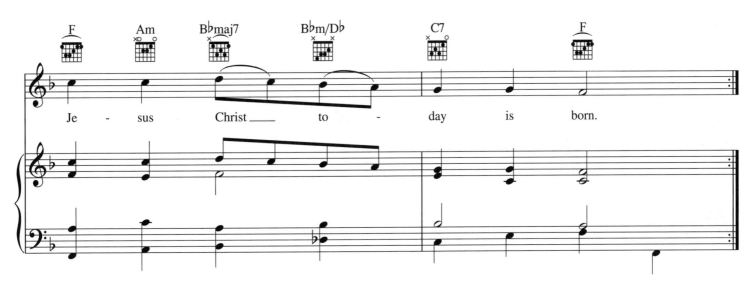

Je - sus Christ ___ to - day is born.

Additional Verses

3. God comes down that man may rise,
   Lifted by Him to the skies;
   Christ is Son of Man that we
   Son of God in Him may be:
   Refrain

4. O renew us, Lord, we pray,
   With Thy spirit day by day;
   That we ever one may be
   With the Father and with Thee:
   Refrain

SLEEP, HOLY BABE

Words by EDWARD CASWELL
Music by J.B. DYKES

SLEEP, O SLEEP, MY PRECIOUS CHILD

Traditional Italian Carol

THE SNOW LAY ON THE GROUND

Traditional Irish Carol

THE STAR OF CHRISTMAS MORNING

Traditional

STAR OF THE EAST

Words by GEORGE COOPER
Music by AMANDA KENNEDY

TOYLAND
from BABES IN TOYLAND

Words by GLEN MacDONOUGH
Music by VICTOR HERBERT

STILL, STILL, STILL

Salzburg Melody c. 1819
Traditional Austrian Text

Gently

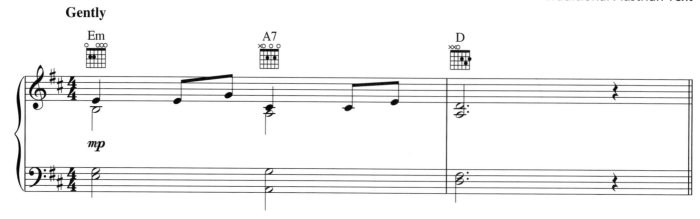

Still, _____ still, _____ still; to _____ sleep is _____ now His _____
Sleep, _____ sleep, _____ sleep, while _____ we Thy _____ vig - il _____

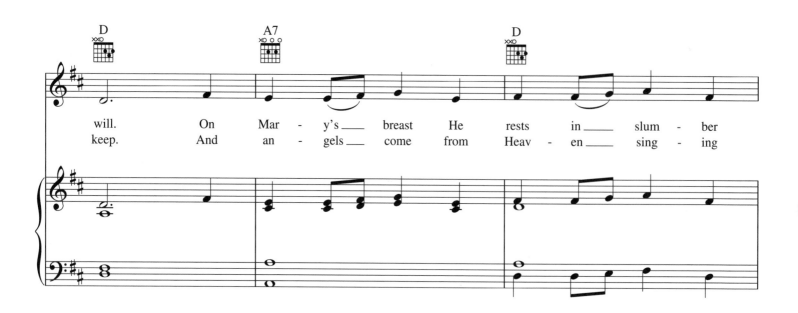

will. On Mar - y's _____ breast He rests in _____ slum - ber
keep. And an - gels _____ come from Heav - en _____ sing - ing

THERE'S A SONG IN THE AIR

Words and Music by JOSIAH G. HOLLAND
and KARL P. HARRINGTON

Additional Verses

3. In the light of that star
   Lie the ages impearled,
   And that song from afar
   Has swept over the world.
   Ev'ry hearth is aflame, and the angels sing
   In the homes of the nations that Jesus is King!

4. We rejoice in the light,
   And we echo the song
   That comes down thro' the night
   From the heavenly throng.
   Ay! we shout to the lovely evangel they bring
   And we greet in His cradle our Savior and King!

'TWAS THE NIGHT BEFORE CHRISTMAS

Words by CLEMENT CLARK MOORE
Music by F. HENRI KLICKMAN

Additional Verses

3. With a little old driver so lively and quick,
   I knew in a moment it must be St. Nick.
   More rapid than eagles his coursers they came,
   And he whistled, and shouted, and called them by name:
   "Now, Dasher! Now, Dancer! Now, Prancer! Now Vixen!
   On, Comet! On, Cupid, On Donder and Blitzen!
   To the top of the porch, to the top of the wall!
   Now dash away, dash away, dash away all!"

4. As dry leaves that before the wild hurricane fly,
   When they meet with an obstacle, mount to the sky,
   So up to the house-top the coursers they flew,
   With the sleigh full of toys, and St. Nicholas, too.
   And then in a twinkling I heard on the roof
   The prancing and pawing of each little hoof.
   As I drew in my head, and was turning around,
   Down the chimney St. Nicholas came with a bound.

5. He was dressed all in fur from his head to his foot,
   And his clothes were all tarnished with ashes and soot;
   A bundle of toys he had flung on his back,
   And he looked like a peddler just opening his pack.
   His eyes how they twinkled! His dimples how merry!
   His cheeks were like roses, his nose like a cherry.
   His droll little mouth was drawn up like a bow,
   And the beard of his chin was as white as the snow.

6. The stump of a pipe he held tight in his teeth,
   And the smoke, it encircled his head like a wreath.
   He had a broad face, and a round little belly
   That shook, when he laughed, like a bowl full of jelly.
   He was chubby and plump, a right jolly old elf,
   And I laughed when I saw him, in spite of myself.
   A wink of his eye, and a twist of his head,
   Soon gave me to know I had nothing to dread.

7. He spoke not a word, but went straight to his work,
   And filled all the stockings; then turned with a jerk,
   And laying his finger aside of his nose,
   And giving a nod, up the chimney he rose.
   He sprang to his sleigh, to his team gave a whistle,
   And away they all fled like the down of a thistle;
   But I heard him exclaim, ere he drove out of sight:
   "Happy Christmas to all, and to all a Good-night!"

THE TWELVE DAYS OF CHRISTMAS

Traditional English Carol

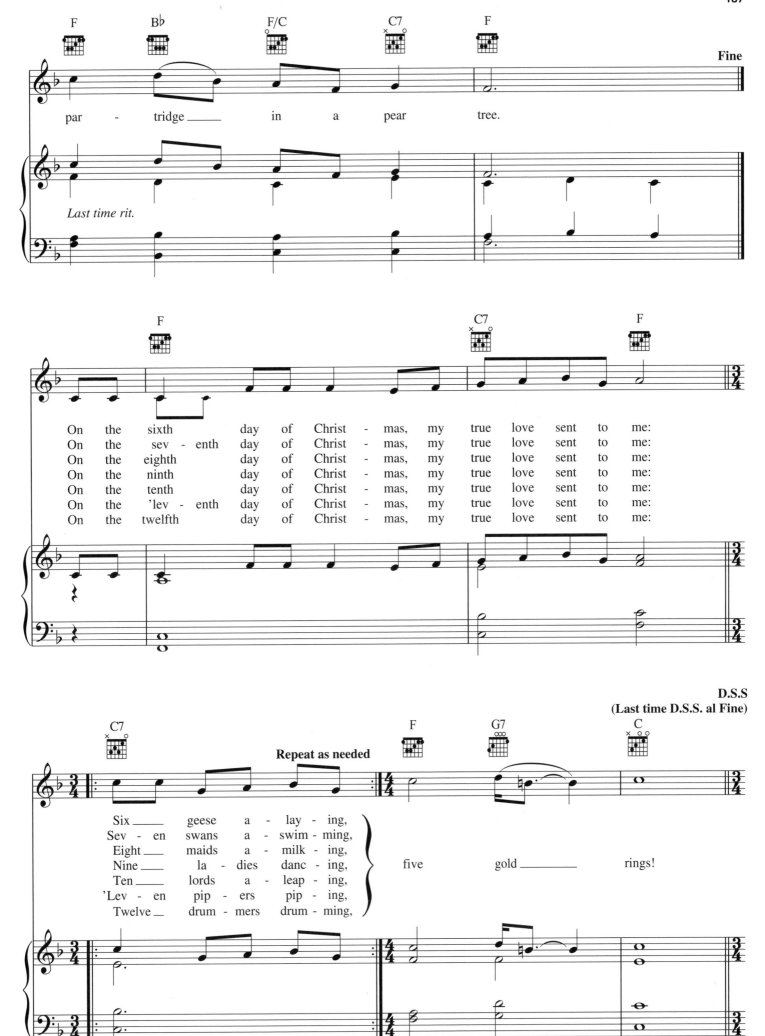

A VIRGIN UNSPOTTED

Traditional English Carol

Additional Verses

3. Then presently after, the shepherds did spy
   Vast numbers of angels to stand in the sky;
   They joyfully talked and sweetly did sing:
   "To God be all glory, our heavenly King."
   Refrain

4. To teach us humility all this was done,
   And learn we from thence haughty pride for to shun;
   A manger His cradle who came from above,
   The great God of mercy, of peace and of love.
   Refrain

WATCHMAN, TELL US OF THE NIGHT

Traditional

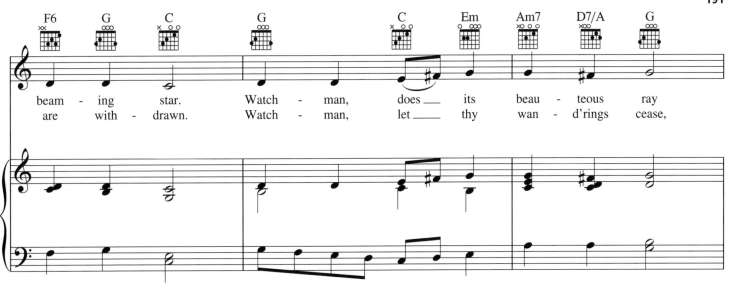

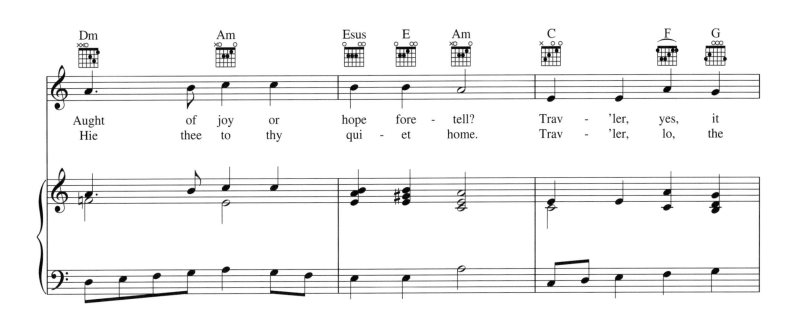

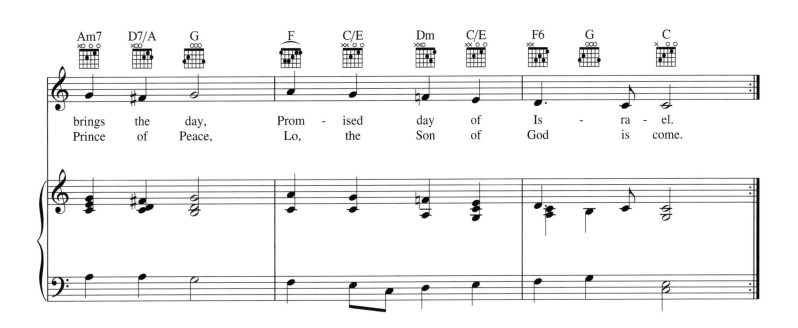

WE THREE KINGS OF ORIENT ARE

Words and Music by
JOHN H. HOPKINS, JR.

WE WISH YOU A MERRY CHRISTMAS

Traditional English Folksong

WHAT CHILD IS THIS?

Words by WILLIAM C. DIX
16th Century English Melody

Moderately slow

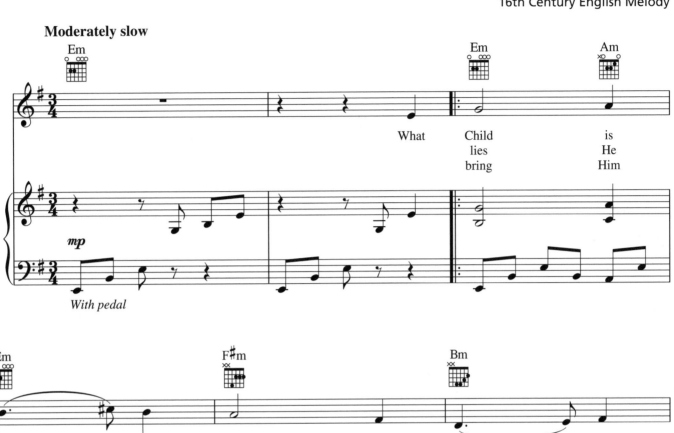

What Child is
lies He
bring Him

this, _____ who, laid to rest, _____ on
in _____ such mean es - tate, _____ where
in - cense, gold, and myrrh, _____ come,

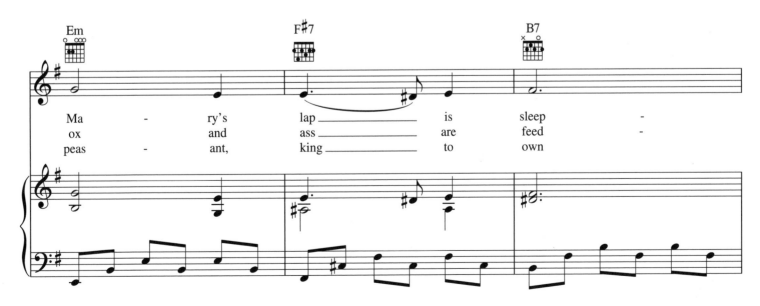

Ma - ry's lap _____ is sleep -
ox and ass _____ are feed -
peas - ant, king _____ to own

WEXFORD CAROL

Traditional Irish Carol

Additional Verses

3. Near Bethlehem did shepherds keep
   Their flocks of lambs and feeding sheep;
   To whom God's angels did appear,
   Which put the shepherds in great fear.
   "Prepare and go," the angels said,
   "To Bethlehem, be not afraid;
   For there you'll find this happy morn
   A princely Babe, sweet Jesus born."

4. With thankful heart and joyful mind,
   The shepherds went, the Babe to find;
   And as God's angel had foretold,
   They did our Savior Christ behold.
   Within a manger He was laid,
   And by His side, the virgin maid,
   Attending on the Lord of life,
   Who came to earth to end all strife.

5. There were three wise men from afar,
   Directed by a glorious star;
   And on they wandered night and day,
   Until they came where Jesus lay.
   And when they came unto that place
   Where our beloved Messiah was,
   They humbly cast them at His feet,
   With gifts of gold and incense sweet.

WHEN CHRIST WAS BORN OF MARY FREE

Traditional English Carol

WHEN CHRISTMAS MORN IS DAWNING

Traditional Swedish

WHILE SHEPHERDS WATCHED THEIR FLOCKS BY NIGHT

Words by NAHUM TATE
Music by GEORGE FRIDERIC HANDEL

1. While __ shep - herds watched their flocks by __ night, All __
2. not!" said he, for might - y __ dread Had __
3.-6. *(See additional verses)*

seat - ed on the __ ground, __ The __ an - gel of the
seized their trou - bled __ mind, __ "Glad __ tid - ings of the great

Lord came down, and glory shone a - round, And
joy I bring, To you and all man - kind, To

glo - ry shone a - round. "Fear cease!"
you and all man - kind. To

Additional Verses

3. To you, in David's town this day,
   Is born of David's line,
   The Savior, who is Christ the Lord;
   And this shall be the sign,
   And this shall be the sign:

4. The heavenly Babe you there shall find
   To human view displayed,
   All meanly wrapped in swathing bands,
   And in a manger laid,
   And in a manger laid."

5. Thus spake the seraph; and forthwith
   Appeared a shining throng
   Of angels praising God on high,
   Who thus addressed their song,
   Who thus addressed their song:

6. "All glory be to God on high,
   And to the earth be peace;
   Good will henceforth from heav'n to men,
   Begin and never cease,
   Begin and never cease!"

WINDS THROUGH THE OLIVE TREES

19th Century American Carol